THINK BILLIONAIRE

285

BUSINESS LESSONS

I0503659

Dinesh Kumar Goyal

Dedicated

To

Shree Shirdi Sai Baba

I am indebted

To

My Respected Parents

And

My Wife Vimla

INDEX

015: You do not know why you could not retain the...

016: The competition's weakness is not your...

017: A customer found was past. Serving him is...

018: The bigger you grow, the more you tend towards furthering your own cause...

019: You will not have any price or product advantage over your competition again...

020: Who will walk in when you walk away from your customer...

021: While caring a customer; one should follow the three C's...

022: "Talk less, Listen more," "Take less, Give more...

023: If your customer loses his temper...

024: You should not 'draw a long bow' while tackling a complaining customer...

025; if an organization wounds its customer's faith...

026: Every moment you spend in the company of a customer is expensive...

027: It is believed, 'all that glitters is not gold...

028: It is said that everybody's business is nobody's business...

029: Giving Service to the customer is everybody's business in the organization...

030: When it comes to competing for the 'Excellence in Customer Service Award...

031: Worship the customer to always remain with...

032: Sometimes you have to handle an angry customer, who is rude in behaviour too...

033: Haste makes waste...

034: Fair words cost nothing...

035: Some customers are known to complain about anything right or wrong...

036: Customer loss! Losing an existing customer is expensive...

037: Every great business is built on friendship...

038: It is not your customer's job to remember you...

039: I know of no organization that has survived ignoring its existing customers...

040: Nothing on earth can replace the customer's place for judging your product's...

041: Serve every customer with a 'smile' on your...

042: A prospect is handled with kid gloves...

043: It is said that 'slow and steady wins the race...

044: The quantity of work done in attending the customer's complaint is not important...

045: Customer complaints are manifestations of shortcomings...

046: Credit the credit of your product's excellent performance...

047: An employee who is unhappy due to any reason...

048: Customer asking for something should not be sold something...

049: Harder the sale you make, greater the benefits you get...

050: You have been in contact with your customer for...

051: All big organizations look alike...

052: Offer the customer product that is tough on performance and is easy to operate...

053: See the bright future in 'turning a blind eye' towards your customer's minor mistakes...

054: Even though, providing high-quality customer-service may not be your 'cup of tea'...

055: Caution! Customer's mind is a computer...

056: It does not matter for a customer how big...

057: An annoyed customer does not distinguish between a big organization...

058: It is not sufficient to have an excellent product...

059: Do, what your competition does not want you to ...

060: You must not hurt the customer's ego while conversing with him...

061: Beware! Do not criticize your competition in front of your customer...

062: Nothing makes a customer happier...

063: Let not your honesty be prostituted for the sake of making money from a new customer...

064: No shoe-polisher and ego massager in the organization, please...

065: Relentlessly improve on, which you have...

066: Have not all features in one product...

067: To make the customer succeed in his business is your business...

068: A happy customer here and a happy customer...

069: Keeping an obsolete technology and expecting to beat the competition...

070: The customer is the king! When he enters in your premises...

071: Resort to surrogate advertising; by resorting to the excellent customer service...

072: A well-satisfied customer is your living...

073: The colour of an organization's bottom-line is decided by its customers...

074: You must take care of your seriously sick...

075: The phrase, 'I don't bother about what my people do...

076: A customer might last you for a minute, for a day, for a month or for the years to come...

077: Bless the customer with your continuous excellent service support...

078: Customer! Handle with care...

079: Whoever wants to feel the heart and mind of the

customer...

080: You are nobody to tell how good you are to your customer...

081: Even if someone is interested in your excellent product just for the sake of his knowledge...

082: A business ceases to be a business the moment it is disowned by its customer...

083: Fire is the test of gold...

084: You think yourself the owner of your business...

085: You cannot be happy when your customer is at pains...

086: Making new customers and retaining the old customers...

087: The customer is a purpose, not a motto...

088: Emotions play an important role in building...

089: It is not enough anymore to merely satisfy the...

090: The conversation reveals intention...

091: Whatever big you are! You cannot escape unhurt in harming a customer...

092: If you are out of sight of your customer...

093: Any customer must have a reason in patronizing you...

094: If you wish to repeatedly harvest the fruits of each sale...

095: If you 'turn a blind eye' to the customer

complaints...

096: In business, there is nothing great but the...

097: Many are sold...

098: A wonderful 'Corporate Policy' of an organization...

099: Tap the consulting power of your customer...

100: Your existence is not in what you get from the customer...

101: For you to have the complete peace of mind...

102: Do not stay away from the old customers...

103: Everything needs protection; business is no exception...

104: There is no 'fury' like an angry customer whose business has been jammed...

105: You cannot do it all yourself to take care of your customers...

106: It is the bad listening that makes things to reschedule...

107: You can be either the greatest boon...

108: Those who are busy today, in acquiring the same kind...

109: To lose a customer on the price may be a compulsion...

110: If a customer demands a feature in your product that is unreasonable...

111: Advertising is attracting customers...

112: Act as a good host when a customer enters...

113: You are good at hard skills. Fine...

114: You cannot hide your product pregnant with shortcomings...

115: Do not concentrate on the sale you want to...

116: It is time to get real. Customer needs things on and where he wants...

117: Stop endless discussions with the customer. Take decision as soon as possible...

118: You are richer now than what you were the moment before...

119: If you take care of your customer's interest what makes you think...

120: Let it be a query, a complaint or a suggestion...

121: Customer-care is an attitude that comes...

122: No product gets accepted by any customer without commenting on it...

123: One must always remember! Dodging the...

124: You care so much and even seek insurance for whatever...

125: Should your customer depend on someone else for post-sales customer service...

126: The long list of Dos and Don'ts suggests a complicated...

127: A customer knows only what he gets out of his

investment...

128: Be ready for solutions not for excuses...

129: Keep in mind that you not only hand over your product to the customer...

130: All of us know! Mediocrity is the worst of the best...

131: There are three kinds of sellers: The first kind is those who are interested...

132: Any business expert concludes his opinion on customer service...

133: Make sure that you are not...

134: Your behaviour towards the customer... determines his behaviour towards you...

135: A business has no pleasure greater...

136: Blatant refusal to accept the customer's complaints...

137: Remember! What your customer has done for...

138: Be as eager to provide the post-sale service to your customer as...

139: An angry customer will tell his tale to everyone he meets...

140: An agreement to provide the after-sales service is worth the paper it is written...

141: Let not you be "penny wise, pound foolish" in cutting corners...

142: Wait not for a call from a customer. Be ...

143: Most failed organizations had one common fault...

144: Gone are the days when it was selling only and no serving...

145: The customer is the only tool...

146: Every organization however big or small is in pursuit of customers...

147: No big organization believes that it shall ever die...

148: Coach your customer on how to achieve the optimal performance...

149: It is not enough to attend the phone call from the customer...

150: A customer should not wait for long to see...

151: The recession is! Your competition is losing his customers...

152: Get rid of having double standards of...

153: In a war of arguments with the customer...

154: To express your attitude of gratitude or an apology to a customer...

155: Use the words 'Thanks' 'Sorry' and 'Please' at the right moment...

156: Put the customer's convenience on the top priority not, of yours...

157: You must initiate an action within twenty minutes of receiving a customer's complaint...

158: The day, you get the first complaint about your product...

159: See an annoyed customer before he sees you...

160: You must reply quickly and to the point of the customer's mail...

161: A customer might not mind your appearance...

162: When you bring sunshine in the life of the customer...

163: Make or sell products that are needed by the customers...

164: The customer did not buy in most cases does not mean...

165: It always earns you more in the long run, to make or sell the product...

166: I am one of your unhappy customers. One day you will come searching for me...

167: The customer! Easy or tough...

168: Customer flies! Be not so loose in your grip on the customer-care that the...

169: The voice of your customer is the description of you...

170: The right to keep you patronized is with the customer...

171: Whether the customer makes you a 'hero' or a 'zero' depends on...

172: Change with the change to take care of your customers' changing needs...

173: Before a customer buys your product; he buys his faith in you...

174: There is no dearth of people abundant in knowledge and skill...

175: Never put a 'Yes' man at the helm of customer service affairs...

176: Be not an expert at 'reading between the...

177: He who is first in price, first in...

178: It is good manners that make the excellence of a neighbourhood...

179: The customer does not want to listen to an answering...

180: Winners see objectives; Losers see obstacles...

181: Nothing is perfect. Products you produce or sell are no exception...

182: You say you are always ready to serve the customers...

183: As the creation of a hundred forests is in one...

184: You are answerable for your customer's complaints...

185: It is better not to sell than to create an unsatisfied customer knowingly...

186: Customer! He 'Makes' an organization...

187: I lost a customer because I did not cheat him...

188: It is said that an 'Open ear is a sign of an open heart'...

189: Seeing is believing. Things seen are real than things heard...

190: If your customer is unhappy, You are not worthy of the happiness...

191: The golden rule for communicating with the customer...

192: Small turns into big. A small customer is to be regarded...

193: Many customers are lost because of the lack of spare parts...

194: An example is not one of the things to influence the customer...

195: Customer lasts with nobody except with one...

196: One of the most destructive things you have to fear is...

197: a friend in need is a friend indeed...

198: Be careful! Your gestures can make the customer...

199: A troubled customer will not rest until...

200: Together you win! Perfect coordination with the customer...

201: Be helpful; Even if there is no immediate profit in helping...

202: It is said that the 'birds of the same feather together...

203: Customer-care is not a new thing; you aren't being...

204: Analyze whether you are 'Money conscious 'or 'Customer conscious...

205: Show me a prosperous nation and I will show...

206: A customer is not interested in listening...

207: You may not choose your customer, but for...

208: Blessed is he who has found a caring supplier...

209: It is said that pleasing all is pleasing none, but business...

210: For efficiency and flexibility in maintaining a product, modular design...

211: You have succeeded in converting a prospect into your customer...

212: To make a difference in your business...

213: Learn to disagree with the customer without annoying him...

214: It is time to do more with less to beat the tough economy...

215: Do you keep the company of your dear child...

216: You feel that you are free to demand any price

for the product you sell...

217: The most certain test to judge the performance...

218: A Need can be fulfilled, but not the 'greed'...

219: The resolve to understand the customers' needs and the resolve to fulfil those...

220: If you transfer your customer from one person to another person...

221: The customer is patronizing you repeatedly. Retrospect! It is...

222: It is very strange! Complaints from a school teacher about your child...

223: To lose a customer is to merit your competition...

224: Light the candle of trust in your esteemed customer's heart...

225: Service delayed is; Service denied. You are...

226: The ending of a conversation with the customer is as important...

227: He, who feels healthy even though his...

228: The Customer Service is not one thing; it is the everything in business...

229: Buying must be made safer for the customer...

230: Every customer is unique in some way from every other customer...

231: Buying anything with great features or with great schemes...

232: The service you give to your customer may not be sufficient for him...

233: Think and rethink before you think that an organization...

234: Getting the post-sale service is the customers' fundamental right...

235: It is important to regularly monitor for any erosion...

236: You have dreamt of a great organization...

237: If you do anything wrong to one of your customers...

238: Happiness is the game of boomerang. Play it...

239: For some people in the organization, 'it is not my responsibility' is the only...

240: Entering late in the market is like reaching late to a feast...

241: The most important thing in business is to earn goodwill...

242: The biography of a successful organization...

243: The celebrity who endorses a product must be held...

244: Being customer-sensitive is like being pregnant...

245: He, who is always busy in combating the...

246: Curse yourself, not your complaining customer about his repeated complaints...

247: It is far better to upgrade the product than increasing...

248: Your product should be so reliable that when you sleep...

249: Customer! He has made us happy...

250: I thought; the profit only was the stuff my life was made off...

251: To give an excellent service to your customer; take care of three things...

252: A stitch in time saves nine. A timely help to a troubled...

253: The value of a prospect is in making him your customer...

254: The customer does not care how much truth is there in your claim for the best...

255: Nothing hurts an enterprise more than the customer loss...

256: There is a difference between a satisfied...

257: A user is your ultimate customer. In due course...

258: It is no use of putting up an umbrella over a...

259: Giving a poor product to a customer is akin to murdering the customer...

260: Who made you great? Your stakeholder! No! Your

customer...

261: You need not have a college degree or something special to make relations with...

262: Customer! When he is good, he is a friend...

263: The real test of a businessman' character is...

264: Many people claim that the customer is the stuff their life is made of...

265: It takes guts to honestly act your own customer and sell your own product to yourself...

266: He who never does anymore for the customer than what he does at the time...

267: Avoid the use of trigger phrases, no customer would like to hear...

268: When darkness overtakes your business...

269: The customer is always right in lodging his complaints...

270: Think and rethink before you decide to outsource the customer-contact center...

271: Invest in the training, your employees need...

272: Leave the customer in the mid of a stream...

273: Nothing is selfless in this world...

274: Whenever a customer is on fire: For most...

275: The impact of the complaint about your...

276: When interacting with a customer in person or through some...

277: Your product is not a quality product until stamped by the customer...

278: Any time a customer or a potential...

279: In general, no customer likes to fill-up a feedback form, answering...

280: Not keeping an appointment with the customer will disappoint you later...

281: Unlock the lock of the net of the problems your customer is in...

282: Organizations focus more on to give services to their external customers...

283: Treat your employees the way you want...

284: In your pursuit to prosperity, the front line persons of an organization...

285: It does not matter! What you sell...

Conclusion...

Customer is money!

Every one of us wants to be a billionaire. But to become a billionaire we have to think like a billionaire, act like a billionaire and most importantly behave like a billionaire behaves with his "Customer". It is an eternal truth that the customer is the only and only tool that can shape us a billionaire. When we are a customer, we speak the customer; we think the customer and we demand the rights of the customer to get back the full value of the money we pay as a customer. But when we are on the other side of the fence, we unfortunately, put away our customer-hood. To fulfil the demand of the customer is a strain on us. It is now the toughest task on this planet to be fulfilled. This is where we commit a blunder. We kick away the topmost activity that would make us a billionaire. Let us remember that we can become a billionaire only and only by caring the customer that exceeds much more than his expectation.

The customer is the only source we can get the money from. Fulfilling his cause is our cause. After all, we are working for him. We are dependent on him to become prosperous. Let him not be treated an outsider in our business. He is the most important partner in our business. We are not doing him a favour by serving him. He is doing us a favour by giving us an opportunity to serve him. He is buying our product to make us prosper. He is our ultimate employer. He is the one who provides us with food, shelter and security. He pays our employees, our debt and bestows all other blessings on us.

The customer is omnipotent. When he is happy, he will make us happy. If he is in anger he will break us into pieces. He is analogues to "God"! He needs to be treated with utmost care. He can fire everybody in the organization from the chairman on down, simply by shifting his patronage somewhere else.

The book presents 285 simple life and business lessons easy to understand and practice.

It is sincerely hoped that the book written in the simplest and unique style; would be of immense use in the reader's endeavor to own a great business or become a great professional a sure way to be a billionaire.

Author apologizes for writing the book in the masculine gender only. It was done so merely for the ease of writing the book.

authordkgoyal@gmail.com

001

There was a time when the customer played a minor role in your business affairs. He had to accept the product offered. Now he has the choice.

He no more faces the 'Hobsons-Choice.' He 'rules the roost.' He plays the chief role in your business. Now your future is controlled by him.

002

How funny!

The customer is patronizing you, to act you as his guardian and care him forever.

003

Anything that is cheap in price must not be cheap at the performance. A product and an employee that are cheap in performance are expensive at the price you pay for them.

004

Your trade is not to trade blames with your customer. Your trade is to tread with him.

It always pays to do a favor than to take the customer to task for the trifles.

Make no excuses for why it cannot be done. Use all your resources to make it happen.

005

An organization is on the track to disaster!

Where a customer is:

Tired of the promises which are never met,
Tired of negotiating for the best price,
Tired of paying heavily for spares and service,
Tired of hearing the never-ending ringtone,
And
Tired of, not listening to his complaints.

006

While 'God' takes care of his creations, then you too should take care of your creations? Your customers are one of your creations.

Taking care of them is not only to take care of their existence but also your own.

When you stop taking care of them, you begin to die.

007

If you do not address to your customer's complaint at his first call, his annoyance will reflect it.

If you do not address it at his second call, his anger will reflect it.

And if you do not address it at his third call, his silence will reflect it.

Wait! Don't be happy. When he stops talking, he breaks relations. He will make relations with your competition. A sure way to ruination!

008

What an amazing truth!

You can believe a dog you have patronized that it will not bite you but not a person you have patronized.

009

Business is a 'comedy' for those who
'Care' their customers.
It is a 'tragedy' for those who
'Pare' their customers.

010

Take the precaution!

Never send someone in your stead when a customer wants to see you. Sending someone in your place will create your uncaring image in the customer's mind.

He will not forgive you for not visiting him. He will start looking for someone else in your stead that can treat him as an important guest.

011

Have no illusion! The customer, who patronized you once, will continue in doing so.

To make him patronize you again and bring you, new customers, you must exceed his expectations every time he comes to you.

012

'Negative publicity' of an organization travels with the speed of a wildfire. Moreover, it is done through the 'word of mouth' which is very powerful. If it gets posted on the social Media like 'WhatsApp' or 'Facebook' it goes viral in no time, damaging the organization's reputation beyond repairs.

Nip the 'Negative publicity' in the bud, even if you have to incur some cost in pacifying the angry customer.

013

You always trumpet!

The customer is my God. I care him the most. Saying alone does not support your announcement.

The customer-care is not merely the lip service. It is what you do, not what you say. It is not a game of diplomacy. It is the game of real actions. Endeavour to implement it immediately with enthusiasm, knowledge and skill.

Serving the customer with mere words might make him listen to you twice at the most. But the third time, he will say 'go to hell.' I have found another one to take care of me.

014

There must not be any place in the organization for someone who is an expert in passing the buck and finding excuses for being late in attending the troubled customer.

015

You do not know why could you not retain the existing customer? Yet, you are in search of the one; who will remain with you forever.

016

The competition's weakness is not your strength.
The customer pays for your strength not for your competition's weakness.

017

A customer found was past.
Serving him is present.
Retaining him will be future.

018

The bigger you grow, the more you tend towards furthering your own cause, ignoring those of your customers' cause.

But you forget that your nest is resting o n the base made of your customers. Be not so busy in 'feathering your own nest' and ignoring the base that has become too weak to bear a load of your nest anymore.

Many erstwhile big organizations engaged in doing so, are now extinct.

019

You will not have any price or product advantage over your competition again. He will certainly match it.

The competitions are so close to each other in price and product quality that only the quality of service to the customers can differentiate them. To win the competition again, only your past excellent service record will come to your rescue.

020

Who will walk in when you walk away from your customer?

"Your competition will; naturally."

021

While caring a customer; one should follow the three C's:

"Consideration", "Courtesy" and "Caring-attitude" to earn; the loyalty, respect and love from the customer.

022

"Talk less, Listen more,"

"Take less, Give more."

"Speak softly and do promptly" not to forget to take feedback; while dealing with your customers. It will flourish your business 'by leaps and bounds.'

023

If your customer loses his temper, you may or may not lose your business with him. But if you lose your temper, he will take it as an insult to him and will remember it for the rest of his life.

He will make sure that his patronage is no more with you. Temper lost with a customer is the customer lost and the customer lost is the business lost with him.

024

You should not 'draw a long bow' while tackling a complaining customer. Acknowledge the problem immediately and offer him its prompt solution.

Be crazy, not lazy in solving the problem.

025

If an organization wounds its customer's faith by 'pulling wool over his eyes'; then it is bound to 'stew in its own juice' sooner or later.

026

Every moment you spend in the company of a customer is expensive, very expensive.

Most waste time with their customers, only a few invest it. The best moment you invest in the customer is the one that benefits both of you.

027

It is believed, 'all that glitters is not gold.' But for me, all that glittering faces of my smiling customers are gold. One can judge the affluence of my organization by counting the glittering faces of my customers with extreme satisfaction.

028

It is said that everybody's business is nobody's business. But it is an exception when it comes to caring the customers.

Limit not the responsibility for customer care to one department only.

029

Giving Service to the customer is everybody's business in the organization.

Make it a 'philosophy', a movement, a revolution in the organization. Link it to your business strategy. Let the customer service be a top management issue.

Make it a habit, not an exception. Create trends in bestowing the best customer service. Set an example; make it a benchmark to be followed by your competition.

030

When it comes to competing for the 'Excellence in Customer Service Award' you must not be the last in the queue, you must be the first in the queue.

031

Worship the customer to always remain with you. His company will make you rise; his absence will make you die.

032

Sometimes you have to handle an angry customer, who is rude in behaviour too. If not pacified immediately, he will damage the reputation of your organization by posting negative comments on social media, writing negative online reviews and doing negative word of mouth publicity. While handling a customer of such nature, listen to him politely and patiently without sacrificing your dignity and taking it personally. Understand the problem thoroughly.

Apologize for the problem he is facing. Employ all relevant resources to find an appropriate solution to the problem. Favour him in giving the solution. Once favoured, he would not leave you forever. He will make many more customers for you.

033

Haste makes waste.

A customer should not be entertained when you are in a hurry.

Better to apologize and reschedule the meeting with him at the earliest possible at the customer's place.

034

Fair words cost nothing.

They earn you everything: Friends, customers, money success and many more.

Be good to everybody to be the best to yourself. To be rude is to be alone.

035

Some customers are known to complain about anything right or wrong. If you come across one of those customers, analyze whether this customer is beneficial to the organisation or worth it to lose him.

Even if it is worth it to lose him, take a last try to talk to someone who can go out of the way to pacify the customer, because he may affect sales simply by talking negativity about the company.

If the customer still is more of a trouble than his worth for you, lose him.

036

Customer loss! Losing an existing customer is expensive. Very expensive! His loss is realized when another customer is too hard to find.

A customer is not so common to find everywhere. He is not found so easily. Finding him is the result of a lot of hard work and perseverance. One has to 'run from pillar to post.' Many prospects are searched before finding a replacement for the lost customer.

There is a price to pay for this, and that price is too high as compared to the price for retaining the customer.

037

Every great business is built on friendship. But there is no scope for your 'Fair-weather friendship' with your customer. It has to be an 'all-weather friendship' with him.

038

It is not your customer's job to remember you; it is your job to remember him. Ask your customer regularly if he is facing any problem. Even if there is no problem; it will increase your trust in him.

039

I know of no organization that has survived ignoring its existing customers and running after the new customers. Ignorance of them has made many organizations 'fall like nine pins.'

The secret of getting ahead in business is to start loving every customer.

040

Nothing on earth can replace the customer's place for judging your product's performance.

041

Serve every customer with a 'smile' on your face. It makes a difference. A person with a 'smiling face' attracts the customer the most. Serving customer with 'smile' is half the battle won.

Let not someone, not having a smiling face deal with the customers.

042

A prospect is handled with kid gloves and great respect to make him a customer. Unfortunately, the existing customers are not treated in the same manner.

You ought to treat your each and every existing customer the same way, you treat a prospect.

No doubt, every new customer is a feather in your cap but each old customer is already a jewel in your crown.

043

It is said that 'slow and steady wins the race.' But this does not apply to business. One cannot win a horse-race with the donkey's pace. He must be swift in giving service to the customer. He has to race to the potential customer 'firing on his all cylinders' before your competition does it.

044

The quantity of work done in attending the customer's complaint is not important. Important is, the work done is effective and truly helpful in resolving his complaint promptly.

Please remember!

The customer is not ready to bear the long hours for fixing his problem; he is ready only for immediate results.

For a customer, he serves nothing to him, whose service does not give prompt results.

He has no advantage over the one whose service doesn't satisfy his customers at all.

045

Customer complaints are manifestations of shortcomings in your product at the customer's cost. The moment you desire to know the weaknesses in what you sell and produce is the first step; you have taken towards caring your customers.

Look not the complaining customer as 'a thorn in your eye'; but rather be obliged to the customer for letting you know the "Achilles' heel" in your product that too at his own cost.

What else can he offer you better than this? He deserves to be treated with the great respect.

046

Credit the credit of your product's excellent performance in your customer's account to make sure that he comes back to you for his next requirement.

047

An employee who is unhappy due to any reason should be avoided to attend to a customer. He will never be able to bring out his best to serve the customer.

048

Customer asking for something should not be sold something.

Most customers are not precise in their requirements. Make the customer understand his precise need and then give him the best that suits him the most, at the best price.

049

Harder the sale you make, greater the benefits you get. Each hard sale will gift you the experience that is greater than the total experience of dozens of easy sales. A hard sale is a great source of learning.

050

You have been in contact with your customer for many years. Look back if you have ever given him a valuable suggestion.

051

All big organizations look alike. It is only the difference in its people's perspective towards the customer that makes it stand out from the rest. This attitude is the stuff that the organization is made of.

The people of an extraordinary organization have an extraordinary affirmative approach towards the service to their customers. They are the strength of the organization.

052

Offer the customer product that is tough on performance and is easy to operate, not the one that also is tough in performance but is difficult to operate. This will make the customer buy the product from you, not from your competition.

053

See the bright future in 'turning a blind eye' towards your customer's minor mistakes.

054

Even though, providing high-quality customer-service may not be your 'cup of tea' but you have to drink it. Make it 'a virtue out of necessity' if you want to keep your business alive.

055

Caution! Customer's mind is a computer. It is highly susceptible to competition-virus getting your file corrupted in it. Use super customer-care as the fire-wall against the competition-virus.

056

It does not matter for a customer how big or small an organization is, as long as its product performs well at his premises.

057

An annoyed customer does not distinguish between a big organization and a small organization. He hammers the both in the same manner.

058

It is not sufficient to have an excellent product and the excellent customer service facilities.

In addition to it, having the excellent people to give the excellent service to the customers is necessary.

The excellent customer service given by the people with the 'excellent customer caring attitude' will not only result in the excellent product performance but also result in establishing the excellent business relations with him.

059

Do, what your competition does not want you to do. That is, strive to give every customer an excellent product with an excellent customer service.

It should be so excellent that a mere mention of it by your customer, in front of your competition sends him diving for a cover.

060

You must not hurt the customer's ego while conversing with him.

Take extreme care for not using any trigger word. The use of it may work him as 'a red rag to a bull.' It can annoy him to the extent that he acts like 'a bull in a china shop' completely damaging your business with him.

061

Beware!

Do not criticize your competition in front of your customer. Think twice about your superiority to your competition before switching over to criticism. Criticizing your competition in front of a customer is extremely harmful to your business. This indirectly promotes the competition in your customer's mind. Speaking ill of him will make the customer sick. He becomes suspicious about you also and starts thinking about the competition.

062

Nothing makes a customer happier than watching the product you have given him performing at its best at his premises. Your product's excellent performance is the best way to retain the customer.

Its excellent performance is an assurance to get repeat orders.

Lesser is the troubles; happier is the customer.

063

Let not your honesty be prostituted for the sake of making money from a new customer. 'Be honest', while dealing with him. Honesty still stands the best policy in the all spheres of life. Focus on making a customer, not a sale. Let it not be the end of it.

Give him owner's pride in associating with you by handing over him an excellent product with an excellent customer care. He must boast your product and customer service he owns; to everyone he meets, to get you many more customers.

064

No shoe-polisher and ego massager in the organization, please. They are not doing any good to the organization but to themselves. They are the biggest source of polluting the organization's environment.

They are highly selfish and will certainly bite you the moment they get a better chance to meet their own means.

Politely tell them to polish the interpersonal and customer relations or leave the organization.

If you are still fond of such persons, don't invest heavily in them. You can get the best shoe-polisher and ego massager at a very low cost. He will prove highly beneficial to your personality and health by doing both the things at the same time.

Caution! Keep him away from your personal and professional affairs.

065

Relentlessly improve on, which you have. Stay ahead with technology. Make it continuously better over the previous one to leave your competition behind.

066

Have not all features in one product. The features required by one customer might not be required by another customer. A product abundant in features is worth only the features that benefit the customer. A visually challenged person will not wish to pay for the camera in a cell-phone.

067

To make the customer succeed in his business is your business. Give him a great future. Empower him with a product and service that enables him to do his best to beat the tough economy. Let it be understood! When your customer gets success, you get it first.

068

A happy customer here and a happy customer there;
Pretty soon you are surrounded by a lot of customers.

069

Keeping an obsolete technology and expecting to beat
the competition, is like 'flogging a dead horse.'

070

The customer is the king!
When he enters in your premises, everybody in the
organization should treat him with the utmost
politeness and care.

071

Resort to surrogate advertising; by resorting to the excellent customer service. Cut expenditure on paid advertising and invest more on providing the excellent customer service to create more and more satisfied customers. The cost of making 'an extremely satisfied customer' is nothing, as compared to the business he brings in lieu of it.

072

A well-satisfied customer is your living advertiser. He is the best marketing manager. He sells for you that too free of cost. He earns you many times more than what you invest in him. He uses the power of the 'Word of Mouth Marketing' which is mightier than the best of highly paid advertisements. He not only comes back to you but also recommends you to his friends and even insists them to buy from you.

073

The colour of an organization's bottom-line is decided by its customers.

As a rule, the happy customer not only shines your name but also blackens your bottom line.

Any organization that is not making its customers happy must live with its bottom-line in red.

074

You must take care of your seriously sick customer immediately to keep yourself alive. He urgently needs a dose of 'Excellent Customer-care' to survive.

If you don't have time to give it, your competition has ample time to give it. He is lurking nearby with the dose. That dose of timely care will not only save your sick customer but also will take him out of your business forever.

075

The phrase, 'I don't bother about what my people do as long as they sell my product' must be negated with no, a big "No".

Change the phrase to, 'I do not bother what my people do, as long as they make my customers happy and get them back time and again.

076

A customer might last you for a minute, for a day, for a month or for the years to come. It depends on how you make him feel every time he interacts with you.

077

Bless the customer with your continuous excellent service support, and he will bless you with his eternal patronage.

078

Customer! Handle with care. The customer is not a laughing matter. Take no liberty with the customer. The customer is much too serious a thing to be 'played second fiddle.' He cannot be left to a naive.

079

Whoever wants to feel the heart and mind of the customer; he should learn the art of reading the body language and clearly listening to what he doesn't say.

A firm handshake from a customer is a sign of his   firm confidence in you. Smiling and making eye contact means he is interested in talking to you.

080

You are nobody to tell how good you are to your customer. The customer is your boss. He only can define what you are.

Your greatness is in a great opinion your customer has about you. His voice is the description of you and of the organization you belong to.

Listen to it loudly and clearly.

081

Even if someone is interested in your excellent product just for the sake of his knowledge; you still stand to gain in entertaining him.

He will tell about it to the people he meets who are with the same professional feathers.

082

A business ceases to be a business the moment it is disowned by its customer. It will stop running and will ultimately die on its own.

083

Fire is the test of gold;
The customer's adversity is your test.

084

You think yourself the owner of your business. You will run it the way you want.

Make no mistake!

It is a fatalistic attitude for your own existence. In fact, it is owned by your customer. It is run by him and the way he wants.

His wish is a command which cannot be changed by you without his permission. It has to be obeyed. You have to align the business with his wish to keep it running.

085

You cannot be happy when your customer is at pains. Seeing him at pains should make you writhe in agony.

086

Making new customers and retaining the old customers is the "Mantra" for success in any business. This can be achieved only through the excellent customer service by giving him more than what you take from him.

The customer gave you the best he could give you. Now you have to give him more than what you took. Taking more and giving less in lieu of it amounts to cheating.

087

The customer is a purpose, not a motto. Only the organizations that treat its customers as a purpose, not a motive prevail.

088

Emotions play an important role in building your strong relations with your customer. Take care of his emotions and he will take care of your retention with him forever. He will become your loyal customer.

A loyal customer is more valuable than a satisfied customer. He buys more of your products, doesn't mind paying little more. He pays more attention to what you say, follows your advice and recommends you to others. He becomes your real potent marketing manager.

089

It is not enough anymore to merely satisfy the customer by having his expectations just met. You have to exceed the customer's expectations to exceed your own expectations.

090

The conversation reveals intention. People can feel your intention from the style of your conversation.

Be honest in your intention while talking to a customer. Talk in terms of his interest by choosing the right words with the right accent to get the right results.

091

Whatever big you are!

You cannot escape unhurt in harming a customer. You will get bruised at least in wounding him.

092

If you are out of sight of your customer; you are out of his mind also. Be in continuous touch with him even if he has no problem.

A customer is also lost because of the long absence of your communication with him. Communicate with him frequently to remind your presence in his mind.

Maintain your communication system in excellent condition. It must respond at the touch of a button. Take advantage of the latest and more efficient 'Communication Technology' to remain in touch with the customer.

093

Any customer must have a reason in patronizing you. Now you ought to justify his decision that he was right in doing so.

094

If you wish to repeatedly harvest the fruits of each sale, you seed then you have to do the work that of a farmer. Nurture the 'seed of each sale' at every stage the way he does.

095

If you 'turn a blind eye' to the customer complaints; he will 'turn a deaf ear' to all your requests for doing further business with you; even if you earnestly apologize for your past misdeeds. He will rather buy from your competition than obliging you.

Turn your face but not a blind eye towards the complaints of your customer, to keep your competition behind.

096

In business, there is nothing great but the customer. For the customer there is nothing great but the excellent performance of the product, he has acquired.

097

Many are sold!
After experiencing the after-sales service you render to the customers.

098

A wonderful 'Corporate Policy' of an organization:
I will endeavor to; show leadership through advancing my customer not through advancing myself.
Make my every customer a flag bearer for my name. Let him be proud of me rather me proud of him.

099

Tap the consulting power of your customer. He is the most powerful consultant on earth to give you information on the performance of your product. The best part is, this invaluable information is available at no cost and that too straight from the "horse's mouth." Use his consulting power as a telescope to have the deeper insight into the problems to be addressed and the improvements required that will not let the problems recur in the product.

 Keep meeting your customers. The more you meet them the more you get the information.

Customer's vision is the best vision to get your product examined.

100

Your existence is not in what you get from the customer; it is more in what you give him. You make a living by what you get. But you make a life by what you give.

101

For you to have the complete peace of mind,
You have to give your customer a sound sleep.

102

Do not stay away from the old customers in running after the new ones. Existing happy customer is your main source of profit. He is easy to deal with than a new customer. Retaining him is gaining repeat business. Repeat business more profit.

103

Everything needs protection; business is no exception. It is to be protected against the invasion of competition and recession. Only a strong wall made of the loyal customers can protect it from the both of them.

You can protect your business only by protecting your customer's interest. You are safer when your customer is safe.

104

There is no 'fury' like an angry customer whose business has been jammed because of the non-performance of the product given by you. Put out the 'flame' of his disappointment quickly before it becomes a fire of fury.

105

You cannot do it all yourself to take care of your customers. You have to enlist people to help you. The people you enlist are worth only the attitude they have, not the great knowledge and skill they have acquired. The best of the wages and the working conditions you provide them are all a waste if they do not possess a helping attitude towards the customers.

Look out for them for their strong will to care customers. Do not look for medals degrees or diplomas they are decorated with.

106

It is the bad listening that makes things to reschedule, retype, re-talk, and redo. Effective listening means doing the things right by listening to them right the first time.

107

You can be either the greatest boon or the greatest bane for your customer indeed.

It depends on whether you make him a victor or a victim.

108

Those who are busy today, in acquiring the same kind of business have the sole purpose of killing competition.

They are readying themselves for fleecing the customers tomorrow.

109

To lose a customer on the price may be a compulsion. But to lose him because of neglect in after-sales service is a gross mistake.

There can be no comparison between the two in losing the customer.

110

If a customer demands a feature in your product that is unreasonable in your view, think again. It could be a multimillion innovative idea.

A wise and innovative customer's requirements are always unique. Fulfilling these requirements makes your product different from others. It will bring you more business and will make you rich.

111

Advertising is attracting customers.

Customer service is retaining them.

112

Act as a good host when a customer enters and leaves your premises irrespective of, he makes or doesn't make a purchase. Treat him as a great guest the way you would have treated someone special in the party hosted by you.

A well-greeted customer is half won. Make him 'feel at home.' Your interaction with him should make him feel as if he is dealing with his own company.

An uncomfortable customer makes the limited communication and tends to make an early exit.

113

You are good at hard skills. Fine! But you must be excellent at soft skills too to avoid appointments turn into disappointments.

114

You cannot hide your product pregnant with shortcomings. This cannot be hidden for a long time. The customer would come to know of it sooner or later.

115

Do not concentrate on the sale you want to make. Focus on the solution to the customer's requirements and the sale will automatically follow.

116

It is time to get real. Customer needs things on and where he wants. Your product must be available in the customer's vicinity to make him buy the best product, at the best price with the best customer service. Do it at once. Delay breeds loss in business. The rapidity with which the customer shifts to your competition is astonishing.

Immediately ask yourself, where do I stand in caring my customers? How can I serve them cheaper, better and faster? Think of local service support. That could be an answer.

117

Stop endless discussions with the customer. Take decision as soon as possible. Before you decide to keep him with you, he might have decided to leave you.

118

You are richer now than what you were the moment

before; if you have made a customer smile with joy.

119

If you take care of your customer's interest what makes you think that he will not take care of your interests.

120

Let it be a query, a complaint or a suggestion?
Pay equal attention to each of them.

121

Customer-care is an attitude that comes solely from you being customer sensitive.

For a customer sensitive organization, there is neither a greater reward than the customer satisfaction nor a greater punishment than the customer frustration.

It feels an earthquake when its customer feels a tremor.

122

No product gets accepted by any customer without commenting on it. Listen to his comments which are valuable suggestions. You will be amazed at the suggestions you get on the improvements you need to implement in the product.

123

One must always remember!
Dodging the responsibilities towards the customers does not dodge its consequences.

124

You care so much and even seek insurance for whatever is precious and dear to you. But why, this is an exception to your customer who you claim to be the most precious and dear to you.
Let him at least seek your firm assurance that he will be taken care of by you at all times, be it good or bad.

125

Should your customer depend on someone else for post-sales customer service? If "Yes", then you will not be long in the business you are in. Selling without intention to give after-sales customer service is swindling.

126

The long list of Dos and Don'ts suggests a complicated and inferior product. More complicated the product, the more problems. Minimize Dos and Don'ts to maximize customer's confidence in your product.

127

A customer knows only what he gets out of his investment. He must get back more than what he gives. Maximize the customer's return on his investment hour after hour, day after day and year after year.

128

Be ready for solutions not for excuses. Most people find excuses to keep away from imparting the after-sales customer service.

He who makes excuses now will accuse himself later. Every excuse made is a nail in the coffin of his business.

129

Keep in mind that you not only hand over your product to the customer but also your self-respect in the form of promise you make.

To stand well in his eyes, you must walk the talk.

The customer pays not only for the product but also for the promise you make.

A promise made is the debt to be paid. You have to fulfil it to maintain your self-respect.

130

All of us know!

Mediocrity is the worst of the best.

Mediocrity in supporting the customers is not supportable.

131

There are three kinds of sellers:

The first kind is those who are interested in selling only but are not at all interested listening to his customers' complaints.

The second kind is those who listen to their customers' complaints but do only just as much the situation demands.

Lastly, the third kind, the most regarded and valuable is those who listen to their customers' complaints patiently. They grasp the trouble and work promptly on it beyond the immediate need; until the customer is in his supreme bliss.

132

Any business expert concludes his opinion on customer service.

I too have the same opinion. Customer-care brings more customers.

More customers hence more profit. I would definitely recommend it to everyone.

133

Make sure that you are not stealing from the customer while dealing with him.

The customer believes that you are giving him the best of what he is giving you.

134

Your behaviour towards the customer determines his behaviour towards you. Your positive behaviour with him will get you a positive response from him. If you feel him important, he also will feel you important.

135

A business has no pleasure greater than the presence of the customers and no loneliness greater than the absence of the customers.

136

Blatant refusal to accept the customer's complaints is not only the blatant exhibition of your lack of competence and self-confidence in the product but also the lack of your own self-respect.

137

Remember!

What your customer has done for you before counting what you have done for him.

Forget not!

You still have to do a lot for him.

138

Be as eager to provide the post-sale service to your customer as!

You were eager to conclude the sale.

139

An angry customer will tell his tale to everyone he meets and will make it believed by each of them. He will advise them not to deal with the person, he dealt with. These people will further narrate this story to other people they meet; making it a chain reaction and doing a great damage to your reputation. You must treat every customer with care, not to make him angry.

One angry customer is enough! Two are many!! Three would be impossible to afford!!!

140

An agreement to provide the after-sales service is worth the paper it is written on if you do not have an intention to fulfil it.

Customer service is more an intention than a compulsion.

141

Let not you be "penny wise, pound foolish" in cutting corners on customer service investment for making more profit. Savings on customer care investment look handsome but resultant losses are dreadful. You will gain much lesser than you save. No organization has ever died because of investing on customer-care but many have died because of saving on it.

142

Wait not for a call from a customer. Be proactive! Schedule a visit to meet him rather respond to it. Meet him today. Let it not be tomorrow. It is always the last meeting you had with him that influences him the most.

143

Most failed organizations had one common fault. They saw customer service to their disadvantage. They took it as a cost, not as an investment. There is much more to gain in investing in the customer service than that meets the eye. You should pare the overheads to spare the funds for the customer-welfare.

144

Gone are the days when it was selling only and no serving. Now the lack of the customer service leads to blunders. It has become economics of doing business. Your best customer stays the best until you provide him much better customer service than your competition does. The moment you go lax on it, the best becomes the worst in no time.

145

The customer is the only tool!

That can shape your future as you wish its shape to be.

146

Every organization however big or small is in pursuit of customers. Diamond too needs a customer to value it.

147

No big organization believes that it shall ever die.

If it thinks so, it is living in a fool's paradise.

Whatever big it is, ignore the customer and it is a history.

148

Coach your customer on how to achieve the optimal performance from the product that he has purchased from you.

If he is expected to do certain things for achieving this, then he must be taught how to do the same things.

149

It is not enough to attend the phone call from the customer. Its response time plays an important role in your caring image in the caller's mind. Shorter the response time better the image. He should not be put on hold for more than four rings. He must listen to someone on the other end of that period. Otherwise, it might frustrate him to the level that you will never need to reply his phone call.

150

A customer should not wait for long to see you on your premises. Every passing minute increases his tension. Sending someone in place of you to meet him will be a blunder. It can frustrate him to the extent that he will take his business to your competition.

151

The recession is! Your competition is losing his customers.
The depression is! You are losing your customers.

152

Get rid of having double standards of behaviour.
One is for, in the presence of the customer.
Another is for, at the back of him.
Only a hypocrite does so and he is said to be rotten up to the core of his heart.

153

In a war of arguments with the customer, it is only you, who will lose.

Avoid it.

If it is unavoidable, learn to fight it with silence.

Silence is the best argument to fight an argument.

154

To express your attitude of gratitude or an apology to a customer, merely doing it verbally, writing a letter or by making a phone-call will not be more effective than meeting him in person.

A personal touch is always stronger than any other form of communication.

155

Use the words 'Thanks' 'Sorry' and 'Please' at the right moment, in the right tone, in the right quantity and with the right gesture and body language when attending to a customer.

156

Put the customer's convenience on the top priority not, of yours. If your customer wants to meet you; meet him at the place and time convenient for him.

157

You must initiate an action within twenty minutes of receiving a customer's complaint.

If you are unable to do so, you better close your business.

158

The day, you get the first complaint about your product; you need to work on the product again to remove the complaint.

159

See an annoyed customer before he sees you.

The best way to handle him is!

Give him your ear but rarely your voice.

160

You must reply quickly and to the point of the customer's mail, a letter or a phone call.

It will help in building good relations with him.

161

A customer might not mind your appearance. But he does mind your indifference towards him.

About three-fourths of the total customers leave you because of your attitude of indifference towards them.

162

When you bring sunshine in the life of the customer, you cannot keep it from yourself. Sunshine in his life will bring your business into the limelight. You cannot be in the limelight, keeping him in the dark.

163

Make or sell products that are needed by the customers. Do not make or sell products that need customers. A customer in a restaurant will not eat what you offer him. He will eat what he likes.

164

The customer did not buy in most cases does not mean that they did not want to buy. That means you could not sell to him for some reason. Find out the reason, and take corrective action to prevent it from happening again. The customer gone could be a lot of money gone.

165

It always earns you more in the long run, to make or sell the product that is little high in price but strong on performance than to make or sell the product that is low in price but weak in performance.

166

I am one of your unhappy customers. One day you will come searching for me.

Alas! You will find me with your competition.

167

The customer!

Easy or tough! It is you who think of him either. There is nothing like a tough customer. He is a different kind of customer and needs to be treated in a different way.

A tough nut could be difficult to crack but not a tough customer. Use the existing very happy customers as the reference to crack him.

168

Customer flies! Be not so loose in your grip on the customer-care that the customer takes a flight to never come back to you.

Customer-care is the cage where the customer is caught. Make it as strong as possible to prevent the customer flying from you and go to your competition.

169

The voice of your customer is the description of you and your organization.

Listen to it loudly and clearly.

170

The right to keep you patronized is with the customer. It is not vice versa.

Remember always!

You are not indispensable for him. The customer has abundant on the .in or .com to choose the one from, at a click of the mouse.

171

Whether the customer makes you a 'hero' or a 'zero' depends on;
You make him to 'lend' or to 'borrow.'

172

Change with the change to take care of your customers' changing needs. If it were not for their changing needs, you would not have existed. Those who can understand the changing needs of their customers and translate them rapidly into realities can only sustain and succeed in today's world of fierce competition. Even the weathercock that does not respond to change of wind is rendered useless.

Explore the change in customers changing needs. Work upon them and get ahead of the competition.

173

Before a customer buys your product; he buys his faith in you. Let not his faith is damaged. Money returned to him by you in lieu of your troublesome product is faith returned the customer laid in you. Endeavour to avoid such situations by giving him an excellent trouble free product.

174

There is no dearth of people abundant in knowledge and skill. But there is certainly the scarcity of people who are good at listening as well. If you want to train your employees on some most important skill, train them on 'The Art of Listening.'

Be your own customer to sell your product to yourself. If you cannot sell it to yourself, then you should be afraid of selling it to others.

175

Never put a 'Yes' man at the helm of customer service affairs. He will always tell you that will please you, not the one you must hear and do for your customers, to run your business.

176

Be not an expert at 'reading between the lines' when it comes to serving a troubled customer. Those who find reasons for not serving their troubled customers bring the most sorrow on themselves. Do not find reasons not to serve him but find one reason to serve him.

Rise above 'a-complaint-for-a-complaint' attitude.' Avoid saying 'No' for you can say 'Yes' before saying 'No' to him.

Step in his shoes and then do what you would have expected to be done to make yourself smile. Use of either of the two words 'Yes' or 'No' to a complaining customer will either make your business or damage your business. You have to decide which one to use.

177

He who is first in price, first in performance and first in service always finds first place in the customer's heart.

178

It is good manners that make the excellence of a neighbourhood. So is the good listening that makes the excellence of communication.

Listen attentively and patiently to each other to know what you want to say to each other.

179

The customer does not want to listen to an answering machine or talk to someone unrelated in the organization. He wants to talk to a responsible person who will listen to him and solve his problem to his satisfaction.

180

Winners see objectives; Losers see obstacles.

Winner says; the customer has grown wise.

Loser says; the competition has arrived.

181

Nothing is perfect. Products you produce or sell are no exception. It all depends on whether you have strong post-sale service to counterbalance the weak points in your product.

If it is yes then the customer will prefer you than your competition that has the stronger product but no customer service.

182

You say you are always ready to serve the customers. But when will you start? The customer is not interested in your great intention to serve him; he is only interested in seeing your intention converted into an action.

Business devoid of customer service meets an early end. No organization dies quicker than that does not serve its customers. Those who do the best for their customers will only last; the rest would be the past.

183

As the creation of a hundred forests is in one acorn so could be the creation of a hundred customers in one loyal customer.

184

You are answerable for your customer's complaints.

He has patronized you to make his life heaven, not hell.

Your importance is in giving him sweet dreams not in giving him nightmares.

185

It is better not to sell than to create an unsatisfied customer knowingly.

Creating an unsatisfied customer is not the solution to avoid the present temporarily difficult situation in the business.

In doing so, the customer would be lost forever.

It would be akin to, you committing suicide.

Committing suicide is not the solution to avoid facing a present temporarily difficult situation in the life.

In doing so, the life would be lost forever with the problem.

186

Customer! He 'Makes' an organization.

Customer! He 'Breaks' an organization.

A 'Satisfied' customer will praise in the 'Public.'

An 'unsatisfied' customer will criticize in the 'Press.'

Carefully read between the above lines!

An unsatisfied customer is more potent in breaking an organization, than a satisfied customer in making the organization.

187

I lost a customer because I did not cheat him. I got the customer because I did not cheat him.

Better to lose an opportunity than to cheat a customer. If you cheat a customer, you not only cheat him but you cheat yourself and invite your employees too to cheat you.

188

It is said that an 'Open ear is a sign of an open heart.' Customer gravitates to him who listens to him attentively.

He feels valued when attentively listened to. The moment he feels valued he is encouraged to establish the one-to-one relationship and becomes more receptive to what you say.

189

Seeing is believing. Things seen are real than things heard. Make customer believe his eyes not your words. Any customer is less convinced by what he hears than what he sees.

Show him the product.

190

If your customer is unhappy,
You are not worthy of the happiness.

191

The golden rule for communicating with the customer;

When he is silent, you talk to him.

When he talks to you, you must be silent.

192

Small turns into big.

A small customer is to be regarded with the same respect as you regard a big customer with. How do you know that his future will, not be equal to that of the big customer?

Love your customer, not by his size or fame;

A customer is a customer whatever is his frame.

193

Many customers are lost because of the lack of spare parts. Arrange for sufficient stock of spare parts before launching a new product.

Take care of smashing an outdated product. Spare the spare-parts. They always come handy in making the customer healthy and you wealthy.

194

An example is not one of the things to influence the customer; it is the main thing in influencing him.

When you praise your own product, people may not believe it. But when you give examples of your satisfied customers in its support, many will believe it.

195

Customer lasts with nobody except with one, who keeps him first and sides with him in all circumstances. And business sides with him who sides with his customer.

Nevertheless, losing the customer now and then is very common even after knowing the reasons for losing each of them.

196

One of the most destructive things you have to fear is; fear the customer's wrath.

Those who are not afraid of his wrath will soon be crushed to death.

197

A friend in need is a friend indeed.

Do not miss to be with the customer at his most difficult time when he needs you the most.

You are the most valuable for him had you stood by the side of him in his saddest moment.

198

Be careful!

Your gestures can make the customer read your attitude of indifference towards him.

The gestures that indicate your attitude of indifference to the customer includes; looking annoyed, avoiding eye contact, appearing busy, divided attention and non-observance; even if all that is done unknowingly.

199

A troubled customer will not rest until he gets the best solution for his genuine problem.

If he doesn't get it, he will go for litigation and will tender his resignation as a customer from your organization.

200

Together you win!

Perfect coordination with the customer leads to a flawless performance. The product's performance is the common cause where you and the customer meet.

201

Be helpful;

Even if there is no immediate profit in helping a competition's troubled customer. It is the most fertile time to sow the seeds of your caring attitude in him. Seeds of care sown today would give you a rich harvest of profits tomorrow.

202

It is said that the 'birds of the same feather flock together.'

But the people of the same trade seldom walk together.

If they come close; get alerted! Their purpose of coming close is not to benefit the customer but to conspire against him by finishing the competition in the business.

When the competition ends; monopoly begins. To sell what you make and make what you sell is a monopolistic business tyranny.

203

Customer-care is not a new thing; you aren't being aware of it. It is born with the birth of your customer. It cannot be separated from him. Separate it from him and he is no more with you.

204

Analyze whether you are 'Money conscious' or 'Customer conscious.'

Become customer conscious, the money consciousness will follow automatically. Let it not be vice versa.

205

Show me a prosperous nation and I will show you an abundant regard for the customer there.

206

A customer is not interested in listening to your troubles. Tell him not about your troubles.

He has patronized you for listing to his troubles not to listen to your troubles. Show him only the results, not your problems.

207

You may not choose your customer, but for the customer to choose you, you must choose your team with the nice attitude towards them.

208

Blessed is he who has found a caring supplier and no one is more unfortunate than he who is keeping the company of an uncaring supplier.

His company is extremely harmful to your business. He will bring your business in trouble at any moment. Get him imputed from your business at the earliest possible. Anything is useless if it is not taken care by its generator.

A customer in the company of a careless supplier is like a woman in the company of a careless husband. She is always in troubles.

209

It is said that pleasing all is pleasing none, but business demands to please everyone, be it your customer or an employee.

210

For efficiency and flexibility in maintaining a product, modular design is the foundation. Think to build the products on the modular concept.

211

You have succeeded in converting a prospect into your customer even if he did not find anything to buy from you, but went back with a feeling of coming back to you.

212

To make a difference in your business, customer-care must be your passion.

You immediately need to start caring the customers by doing what is necessary and then what is necessary plus some more. Suddenly you are the most favoured by the customers, to buy from.

213

Learn to disagree with the customer without annoying him, because you will need to meet him again to get business. One cannot shake hands more than twice with an annoyed customer.

214

It is time to do more with less to beat the tough economy.

Customer-care is an option. It is a time-tested tool to get increased business at economical cost.

215

Do you keep the company of your dear child only when he is healthy and further your cause to make you happy and you keep away from him when he is unwell? You certainly don't. Then why do you keep away from your sick customer when he needs you the most? You claimed him to be the dearest of all when he came to you. Consider each customer as a dear family member, who desires nothing, but your best-care.

216

You feel that you are free to demand any price for the product you sell.

But when a customer bids a price that is below your expectation, you get filled up with rage.

217

The most certain test to judge the performance of the product you sell is,

Ask about the amount of satisfaction its user enjoys.

218

A Need can be fulfilled, but not the 'greed'. Don't pick the customer's pocket to fulfil your greed.

Robbing a customer will never enrich you. A robbed customer will not be found again. He is no more your customer.

Wisdom is in shearing the flock not in skinning it.

219

The resolve to understand the customers' needs and the resolve to fulfil those needs at the right time are the two great motive-forces to run an enterprise.

220

If you transfer your customer from one person to another person, without any solution to his current problem, will force him to get himself transferred to your competition.

221

The customer is patronizing you repeatedly.

Retrospect!
It is your caring attitude towards him that is forcing him to patronize you time and again.

222

It is very strange!
Complaints from a school teacher about your child are the most agreeable to you to work upon. But the complaints from your customer about your product are ignored completely.
Forget not that it is he, who pays your child's school fee.

223

To lose a customer is to merit your competition.
Every time you lose a customer, your competition will celebrate it.

224

Light the candle of trust in your esteemed customer's heart which shall never be put out. Use each opportunity to be with him. This will give him the supreme confidence that he is not alone in fighting the battle of overcoming the tough economy.

225

Service delayed is; Service denied.
You are expected to attend your troubled customer with the speed;
Your car broke down on the way to the airport requires indeed.

226

The ending of a conversation with the customer is as important as the beginning of it.
Thanking and wishing him a good day is a positive way to end the conversation.

227

He, who feels healthy even though his customer is sick, is neglecting his own health.

228

The Customer Service is not one thing; it is the everything in business. It is not limited to solving the customer's problems. It is much more than that. It is an overall treatment customer is subjected to make him feel great in associating with you.

It starts with your politeness, good manners, appropriate dressing, good posture, low tone, a calm and smooth voice, calm temperament, clear speech and affirmative body language that you follow for the first time and then every time you interact with the customer. Humbly expressing your inability to meet his expectations at the first instant also is an important service to the customer.

229

Buying must be made safer for the customer.

The number of customers fleeced every day exceeds many times the number of people pickpocketed every day.

230

Every customer is unique in some way from every other customer, so is his needs.

A desperate customer's needs are desperate. It becomes essential to discover and understand the differences in their needs that make an individual customer different from the other customers.

Catering to each need, identified for an individual customer is the primary objective of any successful organization.

231

Buying anything with great features or with great schemes but devoid of post-sale customer care is a compromise. There is no such thing as great without great post-sale customer service.

232

The service you give to your customer may not be sufficient for him. Ask him, what else is required to make him happy.

233

Think and rethink before you think that an organization, an enterprise and for that matter any business can have an independent identity without the customer. It is definitely not so! If not so, then caring the customer is not only worth it, it is a must. And when doing it is a must, then why not do it with pleasure and liking.

234

Getting the post-sale service is the customers' fundamental right. Protect the customers' right 'with your all might.' When the provider and the customer carry each other; both go forward.

235

It is important to regularly monitor for any erosion in any of the skills that your employees require for imparting an excellent customer service to your customers. The important of them are communication skill, effective listening, use of positive language, the product knowledge, patience and attentiveness. Even the slightest decay in any of these skills should be made up immediately to avoid the impending loss of your business.

236

You have dreamt of a great organization. Identify your vision with that of your customer's vision. He only can make it come true. You cannot dream it leaving your customer awake.

237

If you do anything wrong to one of your customers, you would certainly do it to all your customers.

238

Happiness is the game of boomerang. Play it with your customers.

239

For some people in the organization, 'it is not my responsibility' is the only responsibility they carry out diligently and honestly when talking to a complaining customer. But the customer also is not obliged to give you the repeat business. To avoid such situations, make sure that everybody who deals directly or indirectly with the customers takes the responsibility to deal with him politely on behalf of the organization. He should apologize immediately for the inconvenience faced by the customer. Hearing a sincere apology always makes a customer feel happy.

240

Entering late in the market is like reaching late to a feast. You do get your share but only from the things left by those who reached first.

241

The most important thing in business is to earn goodwill. You are indeed rich if you have earned more goodwill than your competition.

242

The biography of a successful organization starts from its excellent customer service and continues with it. It is an account of the entire organization's affirmative attitude towards serving the customer.

243

The celebrity who endorses a product must be held responsible for its inferior performance than promised by him in the advertisement. Many buy the product because of its performance vouched by someone they believe in.

244

Being customer-sensitive is like being pregnant. Either you are or you are not. There is no such thing as the twilight zone.

245

He, who is always busy in combating the problems in his product, is seldom entertained by the same customer again. Every time your customer is in trouble, your reputation goes down. Frequent failures are always a sign of a weak product. And he who deals in with a weak product eats up himself by not getting the same customer again.

246

Curse yourself, not your complaining customer about his repeated complaints. You are the creator of your complaining customer by selling him an inferior product.

247

It is far better to upgrade the product than increasing the service-people to tackle the troubles. Too many staff for too many troubles makes no business sense.

248

Your product should be so reliable that when you sleep your competition awakes.

249

Customer!

He has made us happy, Let us make him happier.

He has made us smile, Let us make him laugh.

He has made us lucky, Let us make him fortunate.

He has met our purpose, Let us give him success.

He has made us great, Let us make him the greatest.

250

I thought; the profit only was the stuff my life was made off. But I had to change my perspective when I started losing my customers.

To my bewilderment, then only I realized the stuff my life is made off is my customers.

251

To give an excellent service to your customer; take care of three things:

Stay in touch with him as much as possible. Listen to his needs. Fulfil the needs with your all might.

252

A stitch in time saves nine. A timely help to a troubled customer will save you from a potential damage to your reputation.

Solving a small problem in time will prevent it from becoming big.

253

The value of a prospect is in making him your customer. He is an overhead until he is converted into a customer. In most cases, the best price to him is offered only when he starts drifting away. This often results in losing a possible potential customer. Offer the best price in the first negotiation to convert him into your customer. "Customer once gone seldom returns back".

254

The customer does not care how much truth is there in your claim for the best customer care; until you convert your claim into actions, to take care of him.

255

Nothing hurts an enterprise more than
the customer loss. No organization can longer withstand
the impact of the gradual loss of its customers.
Customers are the lifeline of an organization.

256

There is a difference between a satisfied customer and a
loyal customer. A loyal customer is an extremely
satisfied customer who always speaks the good about
you in front of other people even at the back of you.
Whereas satisfied customer is also happy, but may not
speak the good about you in front of others.

257

A user is your ultimate customer. In due course of time,
he comes to know more about the performance of your
product than you know about it. He puts it on the real
endurance day and night. Let his suggestions about the
product not be dishonored.

258

It is no use of putting up an umbrella over a customer; when he is already drenched.

259

Giving a poor product to a customer is akin to murdering the customer. Caution! A murder cries even out of the stone walls.

He who does so should be treated as a criminal and be punished accordingly.

260

Who made you great? Your stakeholder! No! Your customer has made you great indeed. You achieved greatness because he pushed you there; not your stakeholder. To maintain your greatness, you have to be great with him every time he comes in contact with you. Feel obliged. Share your success with him. Fail not to understand how much your customer has contributed in making you great.

261

You need not have a college degree or something special to make relations with the customer or with anyone for that matter. The only trait you need is 'The Caring Attitude' towards him.

262

Customer!

When he is good, he is a friend;

When he is bad, he is a foe;

He is now the worst of all foes.

263

The real test of a businessman' character is; what he would have done if he had a chance to cheat a customer.

264

Many people claim that the customer is the stuff their life is made of. But in reality, the slightest harm to their business gives them more concern and uneasiness than the complete destruction of their customer's business.

265

It takes guts to honestly act your own customer and sell your own product to yourself.

If you can't sell it to yourself, should you not be afraid of selling it to others? So first believe in yourself in what you say and sell to a customer to make him believe in you and your product.

266

He who never does anymore for the customer than what he does at the time of making a sale; never gets any more from him than what he gets at the time of making the sale. One, who seeks an order by fooling a customer, ends up with that order.

267

Avoid the use of trigger phrases, no customer would like to hear.

Following are few examples. "Your call is important to us

Please continue on hold". "We will look into it".

"We cannot do anything about this"

"There must have been some communication problem for the delay.

"Please wait; there is another call to attend".

"Sorry for not giving you any solution. Let me transfer your call to my superior".

There are many more trigger phrases like these to be avoided while conversing with a customer.

268

When darkness overtakes your business, you run after the customers.

But when sunshine overtakes it, then you must not run over them.

269

The customer is always right in lodging his complaints.

If in doubt, read it again.

270

Think and rethink before you decide to outsource the customer-contact center to a call-center. Call-center is no option for addressing the customer's problem.

Statistics suggest that in a number of cases, the customer becomes so irate communicating with the call-center agent that he takes back his patronage to the organization. There is the total absence of the customer's emotional satisfaction, which is a must requirement for conducting a business in the current scenario of the cutthroat competition.

You must have experienced that she is only and only the 'Mother' who can give emotional satisfaction to her baby, not the hired maid. So you must behave the mother to your customers.

271

Invest in the training, your employees need. The cost of training them is nothing as compared to the cost you pay for not training them.

It is an investment to maximize your returns from the customers.

272

Leave the customer in the mid of a stream;
And you are drowned.

273

Nothing is selfless in this world.

Providing an excellent service to your customers by your employees also is no exception. Don't expect great customer service from them if you don't encourage, reward and thank them for doing it. They will not wish to do it provided they know the benefits they will get in return for doing it.

274

Whenever a customer is on fire:

For most, saving him is a burden;
for few, saving him is a pledge!

For most, it is to keep him from;
for few, it is a matter of solidarity!

Most get on the crutches,
only a few put on the wings!

They fly and quench the fire.

275

The impact of the complaint about your business would be a big blow or a big boon, is largely determined by the way you handle it. If it is handled poorly, it will be a big blow as the complaining customer will withdraw his association with you, and will encourage others to do the same.

The same complaint will turn into a compliment by taking it as a valuable feedback rather than taking it as a headache to resolve. Leave no stone unturned in making the complaining customer feel more than happy. It will be a big boon to your business. It will not only retain the complaining customer but also will get you the new customers. He will refer you to many of his friends to become your customer.

276

When interacting with a customer in person or through some other means of communication; never forget his name. Don't stammer in pronouncing it. Address him appropriately and professionally. This will help you in making good relations with him.

277

Your product is not a quality product until stamped by the customer.

278

Any time a customer or a potential customer comes in touch with your company before, during or after buying the product is considered as customer-touchpoint for your organization. There could be several customer-touchpoints in his journey from identification of the product to its acquisition by him.

Each customer-touchpoint is very important and needs to be thoroughly analyzed to meet customer's requirements and desires at that touchpoint.

279

In general, no customer likes to fill-up a feedback form, answering a feedback 'questionnaire' on the product and the customer service. But he certainly opens up about it on email, website and other social media mainly when the feedback is negative. Take corrective action immediately to get negative feedback converted into the positive feedback; before it is noticed by many people. One negative review or feedback can turn away your ten potential customers.

280

Not keeping an appointment with the customer will disappoint you later.

281

Unlock the lock of the net of the problems your customer is in, because these problems have been given by you. Getting him out of the net will not only improve your net-worth; but also force him to beat the path that leads to your door.

282

Organizations focus more on to give services to their external customers who have patronized them in buying their products. They neglect the equally important services needed by their internal customers. An internal customer is any employee who depends on the timing, quality and accuracy of a colleague's or any one's work, in order for him to complete his own work. That makes every employee in the organization an internal customer to each other. As an external customer expects goods and services on time to serve the customer; an internal customer also expects to get the inputs in time he needs to deliver his own work. An organization cannot render excellent service to its external customer if its internal customers do not give excellent service to each other.

283

Treat your employees the way you want your customers to be treated by them. Customer's expectations can be exceeded only if you exceed the expectations of your employees.

Poorly employed people serve the customers just as poorly.

284

In your pursuit to prosperity, the front line persons of an organization, an enterprise or an individual's venture play the most important role. Customer Service starts from there. They are the people who bear the customers' wrath, listen to them, answer their questions and solve their problems. It becomes necessary to equip them with every skill required for giving excellent customer service. In order to immediately help the troubled customer, empower them to take on the spot decisions on the complaints that are not of serious nature. Majority of such complaints can be comfortably handled by them. The complaints of the serious nature only should be handled by their boss. It will give a boost in resolving the customer complaints at a faster speed and will play an important role in making the customer happy; ultimately resulting in getting the repeat business.

285

It does not matter! What you sell:

An ice cream, that lasts for few minutes:

Or

A car, that lasts for few years.

What matters is!

The quality of service you give,

That gets back "The Customer."

Conclusion:

Customer is "God!" Treat him with utmost care to be a billionaire.